Making the Most of Your Teenage Years

by David Burrows

PNEUMA LIFE

PUBLISHING

Making the Most of Your Teenage Years

by David Burrows

Copyright © 1995 by David Burrows

Printed in the United States of America
ISBN: 1-56229-456-3

Pneuma Life Publishing
P. O. Box 10612
Bakersfield, CA 93389
(805) 324-1741

Contents

Chapter   **Page**

1 What's the Matter with You?.............................7
2 Get a Life!...13
3 Body Building 19
4 A Terrible Thing to Waste 29
5 The Most Important Part of You.....................37
6 Choosing the Right College...........................45
7 Career Advice 55
8 Money, Money, Money...............................61
9 You Can Do It!...69

Dedication

To today's youth — the youth of this so-called "lost" generation; my own youth posse, the Live Youth Crew; and to those who want a better life.

To Arri and Davrielle, my son and daughter, who have to face the future.

Acknowledgments

All honor to my Lord and Savior Jesus Christ. Thanks also go to my senior Pastor Dr. Myles Munroe and all the crew at Bahamas Faith Ministries.

A special thank you to my wife Angela who is a "helpmeet" and much more.

Shouts to the soldiers in the trench, those who are brave enough to work with youth and hardly ever get the recognition or support they deserve. Thanks to all my friends, including Idol King, Stephen Wiley, Fairest Hill, Lee Wilson, System 3, Mark Lawrence, Spy and Christian Massive, T Bone, Gospel Gangstas, DOC, Glen Ford, Alvin Boseman, SFC, Brother Vic, DJ Kool it Kirk, Zhivargo Laing, Carlos Reid, Duce, and Lester Lewis.

Preface

Most teenagers have no plan for their lives. That's just a fact of life. Yet the most important thing at any age is to have a plan. Without advance planning, you can't get to where you want to go. If you don't have a destination and directions to get there, you will be easily distracted and focused on the wrong things.

Most teenagers find themselves in this position, so they get involved in a plan that someone else devised. Many times they don't know the origin or design of the plan, but they end up living by it. They contract AIDS, get pregnant, have abortions, overdose on drugs, and die needlessly — and people keep wondering why. It's because teenagers have no plan.

This book is a response to the need for planning and direction among today's youth. If you accept the challenge to read this book and practice these principles, I guarantee you'll make the most of your teenage years.

Chapter 1

What's the Matter With You?

Would you like to end up in jail? Does incarceration so thrill you that you jump up and down thinking about it? Young lady, does getting pregnant and having three kids before you turn seventeen sound inviting? Is that your heart's desire? Do you want to catch AIDS and die from some tormenting disease or infection? Do you ever wake up thinking how wonderful it would be to discover you're HIV-positive? Would you just love to die in the streets from an overdose of cocaine or crack? Is your goal to be shot or stabbed to death as a young gang member?

If you're normal, you're probably saying, "What's the matter with you, man? You should know teenagers don't want any of those things to happen to them!"

All too often, however, teenagers do end up in jail. Girls get pregnant and become single mothers. Many teens are diagnosed as HIV-positive. Others die of drug overdoses every year. Too many die violent, crime- or gang-related deaths.

Statistics indicate that crime, out-of-wedlock pregnancy, violence, AIDS, and drug abuse are at all-time highs among teenagers. In some areas these teen problems have reached epidemic proportions.

Wherever I travel, teenagers tell me, "No way do I want to ruin my life!"

When I return to a town where I have ministered, inevitably a young person comes up to me with bad news. "So and so is in jail; so and so is pregnant or had a baby; so and so had an abortion; so and so is on drugs." If most teenagers do not want to end up in these situations, why does it keep happening?

We live in a messed-up world. Families can't stay together; governments make irrational decisions; blacks kill blacks; hispanics kill hispanics; sex and violence are everywhere — on TV, movies, and videos. Teenagers especially feel the brunt of society's ills.

Something is desperately wrong with our society. As a matter of fact, something is wrong with the whole world.

Where should we place the blame? If teenagers blame their parents or the elders of society, they would be partially right. Even if you correctly place the blame, however, that still does not help. You still have to deal with this crazy world. You still have to find your way in this jungle.

What's the Answer?

Why do most young people end up destroyed? Because they lack a plan for their lives. They lack vision.

Like many adults, teens are not good at planning. Most teenagers live for the moment.

"Where's the party this weekend?"

"Why didn't she call me?"

"Where can I get my next high?"

Let's face it, you don't wake up worrying about the federal deficit. You probably don't think much about unemployment, the stock market, interest rates, or the price of oil — things that give adults ulcers. Your concerns are focused on today — things happening in your immediate world.

Just being concerned about today, however, can kill you. You don't plan to fail, but you fail anyway. Why? Because you failed to plan.

For many years of my life, I had no plan.
Maybe I should say I didn't have the right plan.

You may ask, "What do you know about this stuff? You're over 30 years old. How do you know what we have to face? What makes you an authority on this subject?"

Good question.

That's why I've written several books for teens. For many years of my life, I had no plan. Maybe I should say I didn't have the right plan.

Someone introduced me to drugs at the age of 12. Within a year, I was selling drugs in school and on the street. I robbed and fought with other students, cursed my teachers, and even threw one teacher to the ground. Getting into trouble often resulted in my being suspended from school.

I did a lot of dumb things. I stole from the grocery store and the bank, sold drugs at night, hung with notorious gangsters, and ended up in police custody, just barely missing jail on two occasions.

I know what it is not to have a plan. With no direction for my life, I ended up living by the plan of the street. When someone suggested, "Let's go; let's do this; let's do that," I went along with the crowd. Fortunately, I lived to tell about it. Some of my friends didn't. They are gone.

When I discovered the right plan for my life, things changed. Through God's help I began to control my own destiny. I became a leader instead of a follower.

I've lived without a plan; I've followed the plans of others; and now I'm living with the right plan. Believe me, it's far better to live with the right plan.

Don't Be a Loser

Very few people — adults included — achieve their ife dreams. Very few live above what they expect.

A winner is one who hits his targets, who sets his tandards higher, who has goals and plans, and who eads others. Most people are ordinary followers who ook for answers. Leaders create instructions for people to follow and answer the questions that others ask.

Winners can see beyond their need for immediate gratification. They have a plan that goes beyond the next party or next week.

Most teenagers are losers because they live below what is available to them. They settle for less than what they can achieve. Planning separates winners from losers. Don't be a loser. Get a plan for your life.

A winner is one who hits his targets, who sets his standards higher, who has goals and plans, and who leads others.

Chapter 2

Get a Life!

You need a blueprint for your life.

Before anything happens on a construction site, a homeowner must have a plan for his dream house. He usually asks an architect to draw a plan detailing where everything should be. A blueprint shows the contractor where to put the toilets, stairs, and light fixtures. It tells him where the living room, kitchen, and bedrooms should be placed. After the blueprint is finished, it has to be taken to the proper authorities for approval before building begins.

This is a key in planning for teens. I suggest you submit your plans to someone who is an authority. It may be your parents if you have a close relationship with them, or your youth pastor, or your pastor, or a guidance counselor.

Make sure you submit your plan to a trustworthy and legitimate person— someone who is not a loser. Ask them for advice. You may want to talk to more than one person. Listen to their advice and, like the architect, gain the necessary approvals. Whatever you do, your conscience and your personal convictions are still your guide.

Plans can change or be altered, but it is always necessary to begin with a plan.

After approval, you may begin your plan. Plans can change or be altered, but it is always necessary to begin with a plan.

Your plan should cover three areas — spirit, mind, and body — for three periods of life: your first 25 years, your second 25 years, and your third 25 years. Let's call this the 3-on-3 syndrome.

Your Three Parts

All of us are made up of three parts. Your spirit is the real you. Your soul includes your intellect and emotions. Your body is the physical container that houses the other two parts of you.

Just as God is three parts (Father, Son, and Holy Spirit), we are three-part beings. It stands to reason then that we must plan for these three areas of our lives.

Some people, especially good athletes, plan only for their bodies. As a result, their minds suffer. If they get injured, they become permanent losers in life.

If you have no plan for your spirit, then you may achieve fame and fortune only to die a fool.

What if NBA star Shaquille O'Neal had gotten injured at age 17 after placing all his hope in his athletic career? With nothing to fall back on, he could have lived a life of disappointment and mediocrity. If he planned for his mind, however, and he failed with his body, his future would not be lost.

If you have no plan for your spirit, then you may achieve fame and fortune only to die a fool. The Bible asks a probing question: "For what shall it profit a man, if he shall gain the whole world, and lose his own soul?" (Mark 8:36).

Your plan for life must include spirit, soul, and body.

Me, We, and Them

In addition to planning for the three areas of your life, you should also plan for the three periods of life. What are the three periods of life? To put it simply, let's call it the me period, the we period, and the them period.

In most developed countries, people live an average of 75 years. Of course, no one is guaranteed tomorrow. But let's suppose you avoid accidents and mishaps and live to the ripe age of 75.

Phase One — The Me Phase

Now let's divide your life into three parts.

The first third is the first 25 years of your life. During this period you should concentrate on yourself. Develop everything related to you. Work on your spirit, soul, and body. Pursue your career goals, finish your education, and get settled in a job.

Many young people devote too much time in this phase focusing on others, such as a boyfriend or girlfriend, and end up in relationships that deprive them of personal development. You could save yourself a lot of hassle by not getting into any serious relationships until you are in your early twenties and in the process of completing your educational, career, and personal goals.

Use this time of your life to maximize your tal-ents. Learn to play a musical instrument. Develop your athletic skills. Pursue your career goals or learn a trade. Pursue your spiritual goals or become a leader in your church or civic group.

Phase Two — The We Phase

The second phase of your life is marked by the readiness and ability to care for others. I call it the we phase. This second 25-year period should be devoted to developing your family.

Once your personal priorities and career are under control, it is a lot easier to step into the second phase of life — caring for a family and building a secure home environment. Many people who have not developed sufficiently before taking on a spouse suffer many unnecessary difficulties because they failed to prepare themselves for the second phase of life.

By this time you should have already completed your formal education and settled into a good job and career. You should have sufficiently developed yourself during the first stage to the point where you can focus your attention on your wife or husband and the family that will come out of your union. Providing for the physical, emotional, and spiritual needs of your family should be your main goal during this stage.

Phase Three — The Them Phase

The third phase of your life is the them phase. Once you have developed yourself personally and have taken care of your immediate family, you can focus on the next generation. In the same way that your early years should prepare you for what is to come, your later years should be geared toward leaving a deposit in the next generation.

When you reach age 50, life may still be fun and wonderful, but you are definitely on the way toward the grave. This is a harsh statement, but it is still true. That's why it's so important to leave your wisdom with those just beginning the process. Focus your attention on the youth who are just learning about life. Your years of wisdom can be a vital source of information for the young.

What I have outlined here is just a pattern. It is not an absolute, but it is a guide you can follow as you plan for your life. It is much better to have a plan than not to have one. Plans may change or be altered, but a plan is far better than no plan.

Winners make plans. Losers make mistakes.

Winners make plans.
Losers make mistakes.

Chapter 3

Body Building

The three parts that make up "you" — spirit, soul, and body — all work together to make one whole person. A sick body affects the mind; a messed up mind influences the spirit; a broken spirit touches both body and mind.

Today's world is a very deceptive place. A lie heard a thousand times can easily be accepted as truth. Our culture continually promotes lies through television, movies, music, and advertising.

Teenagers who lack discernment buy into these lies and don't realize until years later the price paid for believing these lies. That's why you need to have a "protection" plan — especially when it comes to your body.

Advertisers convincingly tell us that we need cigarettes or alcohol to be popular or to attract the opposite sex. These vices steal life, health, and years from you.

How do I know?

After years of drug use — from marijuana to cocaine to beer to wine — I damaged my body and robbed it of its best years. Some of my friends literally lost their minds because of drug use. Others had their lives and careers cut short.

As I got older and stopped using drugs, I finally realized what they had done to me. Sometimes the damage is not so obvious — such as memory loss, problems with sleeping, and loss of ability — but there are consequences.

Plan to keep your life free from all drugs whether they come in bottles or cans. Beer is no different than marijuana or cocaine; all drugs are damaging in one way or another.

Exercise — just Do It!

Because your body is a temple in which God wants to live, it pays to keep in shape. If you want to be at your best, it is important to maintain a high level of physically fitness. Like many teenagers, you may assume that because you are young and strong, you can neglect your body. Bodily exercise may not profit you as much as book knowledge, but it does help in every area of your life.

Athletes discipline their bodies in order to be the best they can be for a competition. They attend camps to get their bodies in top shape. Basketball players run, exercise, and lift weights to have the stamina to play such a demanding game. Runners discipline themselves to shave fractions of a second off their time. They watch what they eat because they want to be in the best shape for the race.

You do not have to be an athlete, however, to realize the importance of physical discipline. It pays to keep yourself in good physical shape. I discovered years ago that I study better and fall asleep less when I exercise regularly.

A physically fit person can study better, is more alert and more likely to be a winner in life.

Both guys and girls need some regular form of physical activity such as jogging, tennis, basketball, football, or aerobics. Hit the weight room, run, play ball, walk, swim, or do whatever it takes to keep yourself in good physical shape. Do not wait until you get old and sick to start developing the right habits when it comes to exercise. Do it while you are young, and you will live longer with less physical illness. Get the maximum enjoyment and benefit out of your body.

Develop a regular routine. You'll find that a physically fit person can study better, is more alert and more likely to be a winner in life. Physical fitness is one of the keys to fitness in other areas of your life.

Eat Smart!

Plan to eat right. Some may say, "What do you mean, eat right? Is there a right and wrong way to eat?"

There is a right and wrong way to do everything. The right way leads to God's blessing; the wrong way leads to serious consequences. If you eat right, your chances of staying healthy and living long are increased. Poor eating habits, however, can kill you at an early age.

Eating right means selecting foods that will give you the greatest benefit and advantage. Processed, high-fat foods cause you to lose your health. What's the best way to eat? Studies prove that eating foods in their natural state provides the best nutrition. It is important to eat high fiber foods, honey, nuts, and bran products. Choose a diet of fruits and vegetables, limited meat or no meat at all, little refined (white) sugar and salt, no junk food, and no foods high in fat.

Eating foods in their natural state provides the best nutrition.

Junk foods often taste good but can be harmful to your health. We all love the taste of fast food — pizza, hamburgers, or fried chicken — but these are not the best foods to eat.

Get correct information on food. Speak to a nutritionist and find out what foods are best for you. Almost all food packages now carry nutritional content information. Check the labels and beware of high-fat, high-sodium foods.

Develop a diet that works to your advantage. If you fail to do it now, you will fall into bad eating habits and end up in a doctor's office trying to correct problems that could have been avoided.

Don't Give Yourself Away

Plan not to abuse your body and violate the laws set in place by God.

Why let someone else's plan ruin your life? This person may be attractive, have a captivating smile, or drive a nice car. He may also be selfish — and dangerous. His plan may be to infect your body with AIDS, to get you pregnant, or to make your life miserable. Young lady, you have to plan not to get pregnant.

AIDS is not very discriminating; it will infect anyone. AIDS carriers do not wear name tags or identification badges. If you don't want AIDS or if you don't want to get pregnant, you must decide not to give others access to your body.

If you allow others to have access to your body, you mess up your future and open yourself to problems. Sexually transmitted diseases (STDs) are a reality, and kissing is not a harmless recreational activity. AIDS and other diseases can be transmitted through many different types of sexual activity. If someone who has the AIDS virus brushed their teeth and bled slightly from their gums — and you kissed them — you can catch AIDS. It is possible.

Abstaining from sexual activity is the best decision you can make.

Many people have concluded that teenagers cannot help becoming sexually active. That is a lie. You can abstain, and it is the best decision you can make. If you decide to abstain from sex, however, you need to stay out of compromising circumstances. If you're lying with your boyfriend on a couch in a dark liv-ing room with the music turned down low, your good intentions can easily wane. Do not allow anyone to touch you under your clothes or arouse you sexually.

Sex always comes with consequences or excess baggage. Sex and marriage go together; sex and babies go together; sex and family go together; sex and bills; sex and diapers; sex and babies crying in the night. Sex is never free or easy; there is always a price tag attached.

If You Want Respect, Give It

Many young people make the mistake of making lovers out of people who should only be friends. Concentrate on learning the differences between males and females and learning how to treat ladies or young men with respect. Treat the opposite sex as a brother or sister. There is nothing wrong with communication and interaction, but it is much more important to learn how to be a lady or a gentleman. This simple plan will make your life better.

I grew up only learning to abuse young ladies and thought they loved me regardless of what I did. I was mean, only looked out for myself, and did not practice simple courtesies such as pulling out a chair for a lady, opening her door, and treating her with respect.

My attitude was, "This is me, baby. I am the greatest thing since Kentucky Fried Chicken, so just worship me and give me all your goods. I will return something if I feel like it."

As I got older and wiser, I began to realize the importance of showing respect. When you get married, you will find that a lady prefers a gentleman. You can accomplish much more and be better equipped for marriage if you learn to treat the opposite sex with respect rather than as a piece of property or as a sex object.

A Good Time?

You have probably noticed the that boys and girls are different! That difference, however, goes beyond obvious physical characteristics. Young people often assume how the opposite sex will act and end up getting hurt because of it.

Young men and young ladies are distinctly different. Guys have the male hormone testosterone which makes them naturally more aggressive than girls. The male is designed to pursue. He is stimulated by sight and wants every girl he sees. Most males stand and stare as females pass, analyzing their figures and thinking what it would be like if they could get their hands on that young lady.

A young lady sometimes believes a young man is interested in her romantically when, in actuality, his hormones are merely being stimulated. Most young men just want a good time.

A young lady, on the other hand, is influenced by the hormone estrogen, which causes her to be less aggressive and to want to receive love and attention. It causes her to want a relationship. She is stimulated much more slowly than a young man. Instead of being stimulated simply by staring at a male, she tends to be aroused by words and actions. If a young man compliments or pays attention to her over a period of time, then she responds.

Teenagers may engage in sex to meet their needs, but the result is often tragic.

The guy wants a good time. A young lady, however, wants security and a relationship. They may engage in sex to meet their needs, but the result is often tragic. The young man may have a good time, but the young lady ends up with a baby and still no relationship.

Young lady, you must understand the male mentality and protect yourself from tins syndrome that leaves so many girls pregnant with no father for the baby.

I Use your teen years to focus on having fun and lelating to the opposite sex but not getting into deep Imotional relationships. Concentrate on you and Develop your interactive skills rather than pursuing romantic relationships.

Youthful Lusts

The Bible encourages us to flee "youthful lusts" (2 Timothy 2:22). Apparently, some lusts are particularly applicable to youth. Young people who are looking for adventure easily fall prey to youthful lusts. Bex before marriage, drugs, gangs, and excessive parrying often "afflict" young people.

The easiest period in life to waste time and spend your days pursuing unrestrained pleasure is when you are young. The older you get, the more settled you become and the less tempted you are by "youthful lusts." You must realize that these temptations exist and prepare to run from them. The Bible encourages teenagers to "remember your Creator in the days of your youth" (Ecclesiastes 12:1, NIV).

Your body has appetites. Never trust your body to give you direction in life. If you don't tell your body what to do, it will betray you. Your body often wants to eat junk food and sleep. If you listen to it, your body will end up fat like an out-of-shape slob. Tell your body what it needs to do. If you wait until you get older to exercise discipline, it may be too late.

Young people tend not to plan for tomorrow and, instead, take advantage of opportunities today. They have no plan for their lives and no vision for tomorrow. As a result, they are swallowed up by lusts or appetites. Your greatest opportunity to set the record straight and to develop the right habits for your body is in your youth. Now is the time to plan for the future of your body.

**Never trust your body to give you direction in life.
If you don't tell your body what to do,
it will betray you.**

Chapter 4

A Terrible Thing to Waste

The slogan of the United Negro College Fund for years was "a mind is a terrible thing to waste." This catchy slogan no doubt helped to raise millions of dollars for the education of young people primarily of African descent.

As a teenager you must develop a plan to determine what you will do with your mind. A mind is indeed a terrible thing to waste. As the door to the body and soul, the mind is strategically placed between them to direct what comes in and goes out.

Most of the major battles fought in the world today are for the minds of people — especially youth. When a society wants to bring about change, it begins with an education program. Communists change a country first with teachers, and then with guns.

Your mind determines what your body will do. It determines whether you will do good or bad, whether you will end up in heaven or hell, and whether you will enjoy happiness or misery in this life. The mind is a battlefield where many wars are fought. The mind is a marketplace where ideas are bought and sold.

Someone is after your mind. Why? Because they know if they can control your mind, the battle is won. If they control your mind, they control you. That is why you must have a plan for your mind.

A popular slogan of computer programmers states: "Garbage in, garbage out." Your mind is like a doorway or a storage tank. Whatever you put into it is what you get out.

Jesus, the greatest teacher ever, stated that "out of the abundance of the heart the mouth speaketh" (Matthew 12:34). What is on the inside comes out of your mouth.

Write Your Own Ticket

You may ask, "How can I develop a plan for my mind?"

You need to make a few decisions about your future. First, what do you want to be? Second, what standard of living do you want to achieve?

Let's look at some financial considerations to help us answer these questions. The average salary of a high school dropout may be something like $10,000. The average high school graduate may earn about $13,000 per year. The average college graduate may earn $24,000 per year. The average certified public accountant may make $40,000, and the list goes on. It pays — literally — to educate yourself.

It pays — literally — to educate yourself.

What's the first step in planning for your mind? Decide to educate yourself. Education is not an end; it is just a beginning. Going as high as you can in the educational spectrum offers you advantages. It just makes good sense to plan to continue your education at the college level.

College or book education is not the only type of education. You can also learn a trade that can earn you a lot of money and give you a good standard of living. Even in mastering a trade, however, you must learn the basics in order to gain maximum success. No matter how talented you are, if you cannot do simple math or understand written instructions, you are at a serious disadvantage in this world. Many popular students fool around in high school and then end up pumping gas for the rest of their lives or complaining that the government does not give them a job.

Write your own ticket by educating yourself. Take advantage of school. Enjoying life has its place, but do not let fun get in the way of your mental development. Get educated.

Media Garbage

You must also guard your mind from media garbage. What do I mean by garbage? Many young people today spend too much time listening to and watching unprofitable entertainment. Much of the information on television, in the movies, and on the radio is garbage. A lot of today's music focuses on songs about sex, violence, and utter stupidity. Some lyrics are sexually explicit and stimulating. Other songs incite listeners to rebel against authority.

When today's artists are interviewed on television about their responsibility for influencing our culture, they usually reply, "I'm just singing about what is going on in society, in my hood." Why don't they sing about stopping the violence or how to respect a lady? The answer is simple — because garbage sell... or the people who make records believe that garbage sells.

If you allow the perverted thinking of these people to be pumped into your mind every day, you will develop garbage-type thinking.

You may ask, "How do you know?"

I know from experience. As a teenager I watched, listened to, and took in garbage all the time. My life began to be just like the songs I listened to. I discovered that I could not watch killing all day without violent images disturbing my sleep. I could not listen to suggestive lyrics all day and not be preoccupied with sex at night. I wanted to do some of the things I listened to and watched. Frustrated by my nner turmoil, I decided to change and follow God's lan.

I could not listen to suggestive lyrics all day and not be preoccupied with sex at night.

Every television show, movie, and song has a writer and producer. Producers and writers spread their personal philosophies by weaving them into their songs, movies, and shows. Horror movies are fear-oriented and affect your sleep and your subconscious. Violence and blood affect your mind.

Even soap operas can be dangerous. This demented reflection of life warps the minds of many Americans. How long can you sit and watch people hop from bed to bed, from marriage to divorce, and not be affected in some way? The messages can affect your decisions: Relationships don't last. Deceit has its advantages. Sin has no consequences.

Be careful of what you listen to and watch. What you take in is what you become.

I stopped listening to and watching garbage. I filled this void by listening to people with a positive message and watching shows with a wholesome plot because I wanted to be better in life. After I decided to cut out the garbage and to guard my mind, only letting in good things, my life has never been the same. The issue is not style but the content and lifestyle of the artist or producer. Decide to watch and listen to things that will make you a better person and help to fulfill your dreams.

The Four-Letter Word

Although formal education is important, you can do much with your mind on your own without the assistance of school or teachers. The key is one four-letter word. Read. Over the years I have learned to read many different types of material.

You can take advantage of a vast array of information. Many interesting specialty magazines can be a ticket to a career or may earn you money.

Knowledge is power; ignorance is a terminal illness. Knowledge is progress; ignorance is retardation The more you read, the more your world broadens The more the world opens to you, the more you can take advantage of opportunities.

Let me give you a personal example. I had no academic knowledge of computers. I never studied them in school, but I educated myself by reading and asking questions of people who were knowledgeable in this field. I read computer manuals and computer magazines to get information on the latest technology and equipment. Through my own diligence I started a computer school, sold computer products, and earned a sizeable income just because I decided to read. Whatever your area of interest, it is important to read.

Your best opportunities in life will come while you re young. You have time to read, time to experient, time to develop skills. When you get married, our time is taken up largely by family concerns or aying bills. Use this time while you are still single to gain valuable information. Reading is the key.

As a Christian teenager, you have the time to read our Bible, to read good books, and to listen to audio or video cassette teaching tapes on important subjects. You also have the opportunity to listen to positive Christian music in whatever style you preer. This is one of the keys in determining what eners your mind. Positive music builds up; negative music tears down.

Be the Best!

Develop your mind. Man does not live by bread alone, and he does not live by church alone either. Some young people read the Bible and pray and neglect their obligation to develop their mind. It would be nice to sing hallelujah for a thousand years, but you are not in heaven.

Jesus told His disciples, "Occupy till I come" (Luke 19:13). That means to stay busy, productive, and in control of your situation here on earth. The Bible tells us to be "wise as serpents, and harmless as doves" (Matthew 10:16). Do what you can to gain the most from this world in influence, money, and power in order to make positive contributions.

Make yourself employable. If you want to get somewhere in life, you must plan to educate yourself and pursue the career of your choosing. Remember to read books, magazines, and other materials that are informative. Gossip magazines and corrupt novels will not produce the desired result. God wants you to be the best lawyer, accountant, doctor, farmer, fisherman, or computer analyst you can be. Develop your mind by learning all that you can.

If you want to get somewhere in life, you must plan to educate yourself.

Chapter 5

The Most Important Part of You

Most people consider only two obvious areas of life — their body and mind — which are relatively easy to plan for. Because our spirit — that third part of us — is not visible, we often don't consider it important. Yet the spirit is the most important. Many people care for their body and mind but neglect their need for spiritual preparation.

The Bible clearly indicates that we are three-part beings, just as God is. The Bible also says, "God is a Spirit: and they that worship him must worship him in spirit and in truth" (John 4:24). We also are spirit. In fact, the spirit is the real person. When our bodies die, our spirit remains.

Young people must consider their spiritual direction because it is the difference between life and death. That is why you must find the answers to several spiritual questions:

1. Why am I here on earth?
2. Is there a God, and what does He require of me?
3. Should I give my life to Him?
4. Is there life after death?
5. What effect does the spiritual have on the tangible in life?

These questions can only be answered on an individual basis. A group cannot decide these questions for you. You must decide each one on a personal level.

As a young man I concluded that I believed in God, but I was not serving Him or paying attention to Him Although it was a difficult process, I eventually realized that I needed to come to terms with God rather than running away from Him and messing up my life.

After I yielded myself to Christ, I received new direction and achieved a much more satisfying life. I concluded that a personal relationship with Jesus Christ held the answers to my deepest questions. If I did believe in God, then it was my duty to do what He said and live the way He prescribed in the Bible.

Jesus — Cool and Smooth

Many young people believe that serving God means taking away their fun, but this concept results from a misrepresentation of God. Some young people think God does not want them to enjoy life. But Jesus said, "I am come that they might have life, and that they might have it more abundantly" (John 10:10).

Artists have given us a misleading representation of Jesus, depicting Him as a gentle, almost soft-looking person who would not hurt a fly. Jesus, however, possessed great human strength.

Jesus never lost control.
He knew that physical violence would not achieve
the higher purpose He came to fulfill.

He overturned the tables of the moneychangers in righteous anger when they made His Father's house a den of thieves. Jesus never lost control, however, because He knew that physical violence would not achieve the higher purpose He came to fulfill. I am sure He was tempted many times to bust a few heads or body slam some people, but He opted out because He had a specific purpose that could not be achieved that way.

Jesus was cool and smooth. The Bible says He moved with authority and mixed with many people but never blended. He always affected people in profound ways. Jesus was power, wisdom, and love unlimited. He set an example for us; He taught about life; and He demonstrated what life could be like.

Jesus never had a problem that He could not overcome. No situation came His way that He could not handle. He said we should be like Him. We should love yet be strong. We should live like He lived without the distraction of sin or unproductive living, He stressed the need to worship God in spirit and truth He led the way. We are supposed to have the same mind. We are supposed to live right, which is the foundation for success.

Stay in touch with the Father. Live according to His Word. Pay great attention to the spiritual aspect of life. "For what shall it profit a man, if he shall gain the whole world, and lose his own soul?" (Mark 8:36). Set spiritual goals for your life.

Just Do It!

How do you set spiritual goals? Here are some tips. First, you must be committed to spiritual development and growth. Never be content with your spiritual state. Make progress in every area of your life.

Once you have committed your life to Christ, the next step is to be planted and grow. To grow means you must understand the kingdom of God and its objectives.

Jesus prayed, "Your kingdom come, your will be done on earth as it is in heaven" (Matthew 6:10, NIV). Our job is to learn the principles of His kingdom and to ensure that we live by them and advance God's objectives on the earth. In order to advance God' s plan, we must become a part of His system, which is to belong to a local church that abides by and practices biblical principles.

The next step is to be a personal ambassador and ave your life be an example to others. This is done nly by your knowing what the Bible says. Since we ive under a new covenant ushered in by Jesus Christ imself, we should especially study the New Testament.

You need to do God's will even if other young people disagree or misunderstand you.

Once you understand what God wants you to do, you need to do it even if other young people disagree or misunderstand you. If you are right, no apologies are necessary. You are a personal witness of something you have settled in your heart. Just do it!

I Relax and grow in your faith. Read, pray, study, and witness under the guidance of your local church and youth group. People may accuse you of being religious if you share your faith, yet they share their beliefs with you everyday in song, in word, in movies.

Everyone spouts some philosophy at you every day. Writers have a philosophy that comes through their screenplays; teachers push their personal philosophy on their students. You have a right to share your personal faith in Jesus with anyone. They have the right to respond however they like.

Your teenage years are the best time to become strong in your faith. Many people wait until they

41

have wasted their years in foolish living like the prodigal son, then they come back to God only after being abused by this crazy world. It is better to take advantage of the blessings that God has to offer you now than to come to Him later for a repair job.

Plan to Grow

We live in dangerous times. The world gets more evil by the day. Decide to make continual progress in your spiritual life. Do not be content just to be a Christian. Decide to become a mature Christiain moving from the elementary things to the deeper things.

Guns, needles, suicide, and AIDS claim the lives of young people who are full of unused potential. It is up to you to be the one who stands out from the crowd. Be full of the image of God. Do not wait until tomorrow. Plan to grow from one level to a higher level of spiritually.

You can only develop your spirit by reading and meditating and praying. Meditate on what you have read in the Bible and Christian books. Think abou t what your pastor or youth pastor has taught. Learnmore about how to pray and how to achieve results praying.

The Bible contains instructions for living. This is the only manual provided by the Manufacturer. We must understand our directions for life. The Bible is also our "Constitution," containing our bill or rights and orders from our President.

If you believe in God, you must believe that He has a plan for your life. Decide to follow that plan to the letter. The better you follow the plan, the better your life will be.

Chapter 6

Choosing the Right College

Two of the most important decisions you will ever make in your life are choosing a college and choosing a career. Why are these decisions important? Because you will probably spend more time on a job than in any other single activity. It is important to spend this vast amount of time working at something you love and doing it profitably.

If you make the wrong choices, you can end up doing something you hate and making less money than you would like. The end result is a lifetime of misery and underachievement.

Make the right decisions early to keep yourself from heartache and regret. Don't be left saying, "If only I had done this," or "If only I had decided earlier." The ball is in your court.

The golden rule says: "Do to others what you would have them do to you" (Matthew 7:12, NIV). The twentieth century version goes something like this:

"He who has the gold, makes the rules." That may-seem funny, but it is often true when it comes to controlling the lives of other people.

Your level of income depends largely on your level of education and your career choices.

Money makes a difference in how you live, where you live, and at what standard you will live. Your level of income depends largely on your level of education and your career choices.

Not everyone will go to college or will want to go to college. Some may end up in a vocational school or get on-the-job training in their field of interest, I believe this is a form of college.

No matter what you are learning, you should choose your field based upon something other than chance. Let's look at some tips.

Selecting the Right College

Near or Far

One of the first questions to consider is whether you want to go to a school that is close to home or far away. If your family does not have a lot of money, or if you need to be close to your family, choose a school near your hometown.

Being from the Bahamas, I had to seriously consider the cost of getting to and from school. If you-would like to go home for the holidays, airfare can pose a problem unless you can afford it. Sometimes the school you want to go to may be far away. That I fine, as long as you are prepared to pay the cost. I cannot set a rule, but I bring up this point because it is a very important consideration. Think about it.

Price

Since economics plays a big role in all of our lives, rou must consider the cost of tuition, accommoda-[ions, food, and all the other aspects of college life, 'ou do not want to shortchange yourself on quality, >ut neither do you want to bite off more than you lan chew. Perhaps you can get the same education mt a less expensive institution. Weigh the cost versus Ihe benefit in order to make a good selection.

Area of Study

As I have mentioned earlier, it is important to de-ide as early as possible what you want to study. If you don't know by your senior year of high school, ask your guidance counselor for some form of career interest and assessment test to help narrow your choices. Always lean toward your areas of strength and things you like doing. Consider present trends and where career opportunities will be in the future. Why get an education in something that is no longer Practical or will not help you to earn a living?

College Graduates

One of the best sources of information are those who have gone before you. Your friends, relatives, youth pastor, or pastor would probably be happy to share information about their college days with you. Benefit from their experiences. Don't make the same mistakes they made. Learn from their decisions and save yourself unnecessary hassles.

New Cultures

Knowing the culture of the city or country where you will be going to school will help with your adjustment to college life. The first year of college often the most difficult, and you can make the transition easier if you familiarize yourself with the culture of that city or country and college.

A big difference exists between attending a college in a rural area versus studying at a university in a major city. Institutions located in the city offer many more choices and opportunities. You may have better access to museums, planetariums, libraries, and cultural events like concerts and theater.

A prestigious ivy league school has a different atmosphere than a state college. An engineering school is different from a technical school or community college.

Each region of the U.S. has its own unique flavor, speech patterns, and customs. If you grew up in the South, you will find New England quite a change Someone from the west coast will notice difference at an eastern school. Cultural differences are magnified if you choose to study in another country.

Choosing The Right College

Jr. (Community) College vs. Major College

If money is an issue, or if you need a year or two to make the transition to a major college, a junior or community college may be a good option for you. Many times a junior college is much less expensive than a four-year institution and very flexible. Most of your credits can be transferred to the college you plan to attend. Make sure your credits will be accepted before you enroll; otherwise your time and money will be wasted. You may also want to consider earning an associate's degree first, then pursuing a bachelor's degree.

Specialty Schools

Some of you may be saying, "Yeah, but what if I lon't want to go to college? I know the area I'm inerested in, and there are some non-college institutes hat offer professional certification." That is fine. If you are interested in a career in the recording industry, vocational schools deal specifically with that industry. The same applies to fields like cosmetology, mechanics, and numerous other fields. Take advantage of what is available in these areas. A four-year college is not mandatory. Professional certification can be just as rewarding financially, especially if you choose a field you enjoy and in which you show ability.

Paying for College

Let's look at one of the biggest hindrances to pursuing higher education. How will you pay for yourschooling? That's one of those nagging questions that never seems to have a simple answer. If you have parents who are financially secure, it's a simple mat. If you don't, it's not so simple.

Here are some things to consider.

Even if your parents can afford it, it is important to contribute to your own education. This is the responsible thing to do. Making a contribution to your education increases its value to you and teaches you a valuable lesson for years to come.

Banks may offer loans based upon the profession you are pursuing. Some banks offer loans for those pursuing careers in the medical profession or professions that are very likely to earn high income in late r years. Your family may take out a revolving loan that is renewed each year as necessary. You may want to work for a year or two, then go to school. You may have the opportunity to work part-time while youare in school.

Scholarships

Colleges offer numerous scholarships to students who excel academically. Although you face intense competition for these scholarships, any scholarship you can obtain is a positive contribution to your education.

50

One option you must consider and plan for early in your life is talent scholarships. Many schools offer a variety of talent-oriented scholarships. Sports is a good example — and a very big area. If you are talented in any sport, it makes good sense to get the most out of your talent. A basketball, football, baseball, or tennis scholarship can be worth up to $100,000 over a four-year period. You will have to nake tremendous sacrifices in terms of practice and travel, but this could be considered the "price" of four free education.

Other talents can also bring you financial reward. For example, many schools offer music scholarships. The same goes for dance, drama, and a number of other disciplines. Sports scholarships, however, seem to be the surest ticket. Whatever the case, take advantage of any scholarship within your reach.

Relationships and College

Many students leave a girlfriend or boyfriend at home when they go to college. Sometimes the relationship may be very serious or just somewhat serious. Unless you plan to attend the same school together, I believe it is best to put that relationships on hold.

Conducting a long-distance relationship costs in terms of phone bills. It is also difficult to resolve contacts over the phone. One of the persons in the relationship is likely to feel tied down, especially after discovering the wider world of college life.

I believe it is important to explore new relationships, to make friends, and to take your time before getting into serious relationships. College is a time of growth and transition. Help to make it a smooth one by not committing yourself emotionally.

Some couples already know what they want a can go to college together, get married, and achieve their education together. This is unlikely, but it is not impossible. It is up to your judgment to explore the ins and outs, receive counsel, and ponder the advice you get before making a decision.

Knowing the College Community

When choosing a college, it is important to know the community in which you will be living. Learn about the culture and the environment of the are Since you will be spending several years of your life there, check the climate and the weather. Personally, I hate cold weather but ended up in a cold weather environment. This may or may not be a big factor in your decision making, but it is important.

You should also determine if there is a church or churches in the community that would help with your spiritual development. Perhaps you can speak-with your pastor and get his recommendation of church in the college area where you are going.

Fraternities and Sororities

Inevitably the question of fraternities and sororities arises when it comes to college. My personal opinion is that Christians should stay away from these organizations. In many cases their goals and ativities oppose biblical principles. You may be asked "pledge" to a cause that directly conflicts with bibIcal principles. Many times hazing and other rites and required activities are dehumanizing. In some cases, these initiations have led to personal injury and death. While some Greek organizations mainain higher standards and provide positive activities, any are involved in alcohol abuse and wild partying.

College Temptations

Always remember that college is a great opportuity for growth, but it is also a great opportunity to succumb to loose moral standards and sexual proiscuity. College campuses are in many cases a haven for experimentation and an escape from parenal restrictions. Don't throw away restraint and the Principles you have grown up with just because you are in college. Whatever your standards are, mainyain them. God intended biblical standards to guide your entire life — not just the first 18 years. These standards cause you to win in life, not just for a period of time or an occasion. Make sure you set standards for others rather than having them set standards for you.

When it comes to furthering your education, don't make a hasty decision. Consider all these factors be-°re you select a college. With God's help — and the

Making the Most of Your Teenage Years

advice of caring adults — you can make a good desi-
sion that will lead to a bright and rewarding future.

Chapter 7

Career Advice

The choice of a career is one of the most impor- ant choices you will ever make. Choosing a career is as important as getting married or deciding where you will live. It ranks higher than many other decicions you have to make in life. Why? Most of us spend more time at work than at home. You will probably now more about the people you work with than some of your own family members.

You work eight to ten hours a day, five or six days week. Work is a major part of your life. You go to work because you want food on your table and money to buy things. You go to work whether you like it or not. If you're not pleased with your choice of career, you can end up leading an unfulfilled and miserable life.

In choosing a career you must know what you want. Ask yourself:

1. What do I want to be?
2. Where do I want to live?
3. How do I want to live?
4. At what standard do I want to live?

If you don't actively plan for your career, you could end up in a job you hate for the rest of your life. Here are some key considerations to choosing a career:

Your strengths and weaknesses: Ask yourself, "What am I good at?" Look for your natural talent and abilities.

What are your strong points and interests? Examine your talents and abilities and decide where your potential lies. It is easier to work toward yo strengths than your weaknesses.

Count the cost: Decide what it will take for you get from where you are to where you want to be. Decide if you are willing to sacrifice today for rewards that will come tomorrow.

If you want to be a doctor, sacrifice comes with the package. Expect eight to ten years of college and internships, numerous hours of study, and less free time then most people. If you want to be a teacher, less study is required. If you want to be a clerk, even less is required. You must count the cost and determine how far you want to go.

Career Advise

Focus: It is important to focus on your goals or your career. Don't allow yourself to be distracted. Basketball players, boxers, and scientists often deny hemselves things peers consider important for the sake of their goals. Many great basketball players put extra practice, such as shooting 300 balls before a game to gain that extra edge. If you want to succeed, you must be focused on your goal and avoid the numerous distractions that surround you. Alcohol, rugs, promiscuity, and bad relationships can divert you from your goal.

Career vs. hobby: Do not make a career decision ased solely on what you like to do. Some of these ctivities may need to be pursued as a hobby rather han as a career. Suppose you are talented at art but also have an interest in business. Perhaps you can pursue business as a career, art as a hobby, and per- aps the art can grow into a business. Some things you do for love or personal enjoyment; other things ou do for money.

Feasibility in your environment: Look at the trends in your region and the location where you plan to spend your life. Becoming a rocket scientist may not be the best choice for the Bahamas (where I live) be- cause we have no space program. Speak to your guid- ance counsellor and professionals working in your field of interest to determine what are the best ca- reers to pursue. Some careers can be very limiting in a given environment. Seek an area that is likely to earn you money and be a growing field in the com- munity where you live.

Trends: Computers and advanced technology are the order of the day. Many careers are becoming obsolete today, so it is important to make that choice with good information. Look at what is happening the business community and stay in touch with the trends. One of the best ways to do this is to occasionally read a publication such as Business Week. This magazine looks at global trends in the field of business. Also read educational publications that deal with careers as well as your local newspaper or international newspaper. Stay in touch with what is happening in the world and be willing to adjust yourself to major trends in business and careers.

Formal and informal training: Sometimes you may be better off taking a course in a skilled area than in going to a four-year college. If you have a specialty, you may end up going to a school for a year or two for specific study in your field of interest. A one- or two-year course in computer repairs may end up being just as beneficial as a four-year college degree!

Many schools offer specialty training in given fields. Some of the courses include computers, mu-ssic, various technologies, mechanics, electronics, sewing, electrolysis, cake baking, and cosmetology. There are countless others.

You can gain a lot of informal training simply by working with a professional in your area of interest. Informal education from someone with experience can be a great asset. The little things you may learn from a tradesman like a carpenter or mason ot plumber may be of great value to you later in life, especially when you own a home.

Use every opportunity to learn skills for the future. Little things can mean much in the long run.

Continuing education: Stay in touch with your field. Don't be satisfied with yesterday's accomplishments. Read trade journals, attend conferences, take refresher courses. Never stop learning or improving in your field. One of the realities of today is that technology and methods keep changing. If you fail to read books or magazines in your field of study or profession, you may end up being left behind. In today's world even mechanics have to learn about computer boards and sophisticated electronics. Stay up touch by reading, listening to, and watching the latest in technology.

Self-employment: This option is often not considered or pursued aggressively, but it can be a viable tareer choice. Self-employment is a much better option than entering the workforce since you can control your own destiny, and there is no limit on your earning ability.

Of course, self-employment involves taking risks, put that is a part of business and an integral part of progress. Not everyone is cut out to be self-employed, but this is an important issue to consider. Lacking internal motivation, many people require supervision and need to be driven by others. These people are better off working for someone else.

You may want to pursue your own business or start out working in a field and then branch out into your own business. It is vitally important that you count the cost and assess your personality before you decide to become a business owner.

Your career options are wide and varied. In fact, you will probably have more than one career. A few generations ago, employees were much more limited in their choices. Many workers stayed with one company for decades, learning the skills of just a few positions. Today's workforce must be adaptable to change and willing to learn new skills. You may eventually choose a career that doesn't even exist right now.

Whatever your future may hold, becoming a lift long learner will certainly give you an advantage. Decide today to plan for your career.

Chapter 8

Money, Money, Money

Contrary to popular opinion, money is not the root of all evil. Mismanaging money may be closer to the root of all evil. What does the Bible actually say? "The love of money is the root of all evil" (1 Timothy 6:10). Why? Because living to hoard money can become a miserable existence. However we look at it, dealing with money at any age is important.

One of the biggest problems in marriage is the handling of money. When couples do not learn to handle money at an early age, it brings conflict to a marriage. Perhaps their parents did not teach them how to budget and invest. When these young people I marry, their inability to wisely handle finances causes I conflict in their relationship.

Money is an important matter. Jesus talked about I the importance of wise money management in a number of parables, such as the Parable of the Talents and the Parable of the Widow's Mite. The Bible indicates that "money is the answer for everything" (Ecclesiastes 10:19, NIV), meaning worldly people believe it can solve all problems.

Here are some important tips for dealing with money:

Learn to tithe.

Tithing is giving one-tenth of your income bail to God. Why should you do this? The Bible says, "But remember the Lord your God, for it is he who gives you the ability to produce wealth ..." (Deuteronomy 8:18, NIV). Tithing reminds you that all you have belongs to God. You offer back to Him the first ten-percent before caring for your own needs and want!

Are you having financial difficulty? Do you never seem to have enough? Giving tithes and offerings, or gifts in excess of your tithe, may be the answer to ending your lack of resources. The Bible makes a tremendous promise to those who entrust their money to God. What does God Himself have to say about giving tithes and offerings?

"Will a man rob God? Yet you rob me. But you ask, 'How do we rob you?' In tithes and offerings.... Bring the whole tithe into the storehouse, that there may be food in my house. Test me in this," says the Lord Almighty, "and see if I will not throw open the floodgates of heaven and pour out so much blessing that you will not have room enough for it" (Malachi 3:8-10, NIV).

Giving brings blessing into your life. Jesus Himself said, "It is more blessed to give than to receive" (Acts 20:35, NIV). Offering your time, talents, and resources to others will keep you from being selfish, a trait that typifies too many teenagers.

Learn to budget.

No matter how much money you have, budgeting is important. A budget is a practical guide to dealing with money successfully. If you grow up without budgeting, you will probably take your bad habit into adult life or marriage.

What do you need to know for wise budgeting? Total your income and expenses. Decide not to spend more than you earn. Learn to save or invest some portion of your income. If you learn to budget money from your allowance or part-time jobs, it will be much easier when your responsibilities and income increase.

In order to help you to understand budgeting, I have included below a family budget and a personal youth budget.

Family Budget

Income Item	Income Proj.	Income Actual	Exp. Proj.	Exp. Actual	Expense Items
Salary	$15000.00	$15000.00	$168.00	$175.00	Tithes
Business	$100.00	$0.00	$450.00	$450.00	Mortgage
Other	$0.00	$00.00	$300.00	$312.00	Food
Bonus	$175.00	$100.00	$120.00	$120.00	Insurances
Side Job	$0.00	$50.00	$235.00	$225.00	Utilities
			$100.00	$150.00	Clothes
			$95.00	$93.00	Credit Cards
			$75.00	$82.00	Gas/Car
			$121.00	$30.00	Savings
			$60.00	$30.00	Recreation
			$50.00	$20.00	Entertainment
Totals	$1775.00	$1650.00	$1774.00	$1687.00	

Difference:

Projected Income - Projected Expenses =$1.00.

Actual Income - Actual Expenses = $37.00.

Personal Budget

	Income Proj.	Income Actual	Exp. Proj.	Exp. Actual	Expense Items
Part-Time Job	$400.00	$533.48	$45.00	$50.00	Tithes
Allowances	$50.00	$70.00	$32.00	$21.00	School Lunch
Other	$0.00	$00.00	$20.00	$40.00	Food (Fast Food)
Bonus	$0.00	$0.00	$100.00	$110.00	Clothes
			$40.00	$38.00	Gas/Cars
			$40.00	$35.00	Social Events
			$95.00	$50.14	Savings for College
			$50.00	$20.00	Savings Other
			$25.00	$25.00	Miscellaneous
Totals	$450.00	$603.48	$447.00	$389.00	

Difference:

Projected Income - Projected Expenses =$3.00.

Actual Income - Actual Expenses = $214.00.

65

An excess of only $1.00 was projected, but the actual deficit was $37.00. This helps in making budgeting decisions. You will have to reduce something in the future in order to have a balanced or positive (surplus) budget. This is what budgeting is all about — making decisions based upon information.

This budget shows you end up with a savings of $214.00. What should you do with this surplus the following month? Do you buy an expensive gift for your girlfriend, a pair of running shoes, or do youdeposit it in your savings account until you decide how to allocate it? These are personal budgeting decisions. Your choices will affect your future.

You may want to devise your own budget usinig this format or one you develop yourself. Do you have an accountant or banker in your extended family? They would be excellent resources to help you with this project. If your parents prepare budgets, ask them to help. Your youth pastor or pastor would also be willing to help.

Learn to save.

Never spend all your money — especially not on clothes and entertainment. Open a bank account and put away some of your money for future needs and investments. Learn to think ahead. Save for college, important personal items, or things you need to advance yourself. As a guideline, begin to practice saving at least 10 percent of your income.

God commends the ant for making wise preparations. In fact, He encourages the lazy and undisciplined to learn a lesson from its diligence. "Go to the ant, you sluggard; consider its ways and be wise! It has no commander, no overseer or ruler, yet it stores its provisions in summer and gathers its food at harvest" (Proverbs 6:6-8, NIV).

Winter is not the season for storing provisions. The ant seizes opportunities in the summer and fall to prepare for times of scarcity and lack. Teenagers need to take that same initiative to save for future needs. Having a savings account is not a lack of faith — it is wisdom.

Always buy property (real estate) before you buy a new car.

A new car depreciates by 30 percent over the firs three years. Real estate increases in value each year. You cannot live in a car and neither can your family. Invest in your future. Buy a good used car instead of a new one until you own real estate.

As a teenager, you have extra motivation to make your first car a used vehicle. Why? If you recently passed your driver's test, you will pay higher insurance rates than a more experienced driver. Buying an older yet reliable vehicle will enable you to get lower rates than if you purchased a newer, sportier car. That's a wise decision, especially if you merely need transportation to and from a part-time job.

An older car will also give you an opportunity to learn about regular maintenance and basic repairs. Be faithful in caring for your transportation now, and you'll establish good habits that will enable you to be a wise steward of future cars.

Chapter 9

You Can Do It!

Several key areas can make a big difference right now during your teen years — and beyond. If you practice these principles, you will enjoy success. Here are some tips on making the most of your teenage years.

Key #1; Have Fun

Some people cringe at the idea of enjoying life. Some people expect teenagers to be too serious. Enjoy your teen years. Learn to enjoy life and have fun. Listen to good, positive music; get involved in sports; watch good movies or enjoy drama; party with your friends in a wholesome and clean environment. Fun has for so long been associated with drunkenness or drugs or sexual promiscuity that we sometimes forget that you can have just as much or more fun without those things.

Make sure that you enjoy your teen years because they will soon be gone, never to return again. If you develop the right principles and standards from the beginning, you can let your standards guide your future.

Key #2: Be Friendly

One of the most important things about being a teenager is developing relationships. It is very important to be friendly to others. You learn more by having access to more people. Friendships give you an opportunity to meet new people, learn about life, and have a good time. Learn not to be selfish with your life. Opportunities for growth come with learning to relate to others in non-emotional relationships, Jesus, Who was our example, made friends with all kinds of people. In fact, the Bible states that people accused Him of associating with "sinners and tax collectors." Yet He never became like the people He associated with. He always influenced others for good.

Key #3: Set Your Own Agenda

Many young people tend to be followers, going along with an agenda set by someone else. Peer pressure, fashion, music, movies, and television have an agenda that comes from the ones who create these products. You must decide what your agenda is and make sure that you are an influencer rather than the one being influenced.

Be a leader. Create ideas for others to follow. You be the one to suggest what should be done instead of merely following other teens' suggestions. Decide to be the leader of your social, civic, or athletic group in your high school. Leaders have more power to influence for good. You be the one to start a Bible study or music group. You be the one to invite others to an event you are involved in.

Remember to avoid crowds. Eagles fly alone; turkeys flock together and end up on the dinner table.

Key #4: Respect Authority

Many teenagers are influenced by popular culture that encourages them to be disrespectful to parents and authority figures. One day you will have a family and want respect from your children. Learn to respect authority because God sets up authority to keep order. If you grow up being disrespectful to adults, you can stunt your own growth. What goes around, comes around. This is especially true when it comes to respect.

Learn courtesy and manners because they help you to get ahead in life. Besides, you probably want people to have the same respect for you.

Jesus Himself respected His earthly authorities. At the wedding in Cana, Mary approached her Son and let Him know the bridegroom had run out of wine. Because of her influence, Jesus performed His first miracle, turning water into wine.

The apostle Paul said, "Give everyone what you owe him ... if honor, then honor" (Romans 13:7, NIV).

Key #5: Develop Right Relationships

This may seem trivial, but it's not. Many times we feel that love conquers all. As you get older, however, it is important to develop relationships that will benefit you. How? Make friends and associate with people who have similar goals. This may not seem important now, but it's crucial in a serious relationship that may lead to marriage. Realizing that you and your spouse never shared the same goals or the same agenda in life can be disastrous.

Your friends should be people who are going in the same direction you are going. Your girlfriend or boyfriend should be someone who shares your beliefs, goals, and dreams.

Developing relationships with people who are going in the opposite direction can cause a lot of grief. If you are interested in pursuing a college education and your boyfriend or girlfriend wants to pump gas, that is not a good relationship. You can have acquaintances at all levels, but your close friends should be similar to you in their goals and aspirations.

It's Your Choice

The world we live in today is continually changing. It is becoming increasingly difficult for young people to stay alive long enough to become adults. It seems that adults give too few instructions to young people about the practical aspects of life. Schools offer reading, writing, and arithmetic but little advice on how to prepare for success in life. By following the practical tips in this book, you can actually change the way you look at life and make the necessary adjustments to enjoy a bright future.

More and more young people are being persuaded to throw their lives away. Do not join the crowd that lives in mediocrity, simply waiting for the next party or the next high. Look beyond the immediate. Prepare now for what lies ahead for you in the way of family and career.

If I can leave anything with you, it is this: Keep your priorities in order. Learn from the example of others and don't repeat their mistakes. If you plan for your spirit, soul, and body, you can avoid a lot of grief and heartache. No matter what has happened in your life up to this point, you can change your direction.

Get the maximum out of life by putting God first and planning for your future. Make the most of your teenage years!

nius you need to reach your potential and realize your dream. You'll be challenged as James Giles shows you how to tap into your God-given genius; take steps toward reaching your goal; pray big and get answers; eat right and stay healthy; prosper economically and personally; and leave a lasting legacy for your children.

The Flaming Sword
by Tai Ikomi
Scripture memorization and meditation bring tremendous spiritual power, however many Christians find it to be an uphill task. Committing Scriptures to memory will transform the mediocre Christian to a spiritual giant. This book will help you to become addicted to the powerful practice of scripture memorization and help you obtain the victory that you desire in every area of your life. *The Flaming Sword* is your pathway to spiritual growth and a more intimate relationship with God.

This is My Story
by Candi Staton
This is My Story is a touching autobiography about a gifted young child who rose from obscurity and poverty to stardom and wealth. With a music career that included selling millions of albums and topping the charts came a life of brokenness, loneliness, and despair. This book will make you cry and laugh as you witness one woman's search for success and love.

Another Look at Sex
by Charles Phillips
This book is undoubtedly a head turner and eye opener that will cause you to take another close look at sex. In this book, Charles Phillips openly addresses this seldom discussed subject and gives life-changing advice on sex to married couples and singles. If you have questions about sex, this is the book for you.

Four Laws of Productivity
by Dr. Mensa Otabil
Success has no favorites, but it does have associates. Success will come to anyone who will pay the price to reccive its benefits, *Four Laws of Productivity* will give you the powerful keys that will help you achieve your life's goals. You will learn how to discover Gods gift jn you, de-

velop your gift, perfect your gift, and utilize your gift to its maximum potential. The principles revealed in this timely book will radically change your life.

Single Life
by Earl D. Johnson
A book that candidly addresses the spiritual and physical dimensions of the single life is finally here. Single Life shows the reader how to make their singleness a celebration rather than a burden. This positive approach to singles uses enlightening examples from Apostle Paul, himself a single, to beautifully portray the dynamic aspects of the single life by serving the Lord more effectively. The book gives fresh insight on practical issues such as coping with sexual desires, loneliness, and preparation for your future mate. Written in a lively style, the author admonishes singles to seek first the kingdom of God and rest assured in God's promise to supply their needs... including a life partner!

Strategies for Saving the Next Generation
by Dave Burrows
This book will teach you how to start and effectively operate a vibrant youth ministry. This book is filled with practical tips and insight gained over a number of years working with young people from the street to the parks to the church. Dave Burrows offers the reader vital information that will produce results if carefully considered and adapted. Excellent for pastors and youth pastors as well as youth workers and those involved with youth ministry.

The Call of God
by Jefferson Edwards
Since I have been called to preach, now what? Many sincere Christians are confused about their call to the ministry. Some are zealous and run ahead of their time and season of training and preparation while others are behind their time neglecting the gift of God within them. *The Call of God* gives practical instruction for pastors and leaders to refine and further develop their ministry and tips on how to nourish and develop others with God's call to effectively proclaim the gospel of Christ. *The Call of God* will help you to • Have clarity from God as to what ministry involves • Be able to identify and affirm the call in your life • See what stage you are in your call from God • Remove confusion in relation to the

processing of a call or the making of the person • Understand the development of the anointing to fulfill your call.

Come, Let Us Pray
by Emmette Weir

Are you satisfied with your prayer life? Are you finding that your prayers are often dull, repetitive and lacking in spiritual power? Are you looking for ways to improve your relationship with God? Would you like to be able to pray more effectively? Then *Come, Let Us Pray* will help you in these areas and more. If you want to gain the maximum spiritual experience from your prayer life and enter into the very presence of God - *Come, Let Us Pray.*

Leadership in the New Testament Church
by Earl D. Johnson

Leadership in the New Testament Church offers practical and applicable insight into the role of leadership in the present day church. In this book, the author explains the qualities that leaders must have, explores the interpersonal relationships between the leader and his staff, the leaders' influence in the church and society and how to handle conflicts that arise among leaders.

Becoming A Leader
by Myles Munroe

Many consider leadership to be no more than staying ahead of the pack, but that is a far cry from what leadership is. Leadership is deploying others to become as good as or better than you are. Within each of us lies the potential to be an effective leader. *Becoming A Leader* uncovers the secrets of dynamic leadership that will show you how to be a leader in your family, school, community, church and job. No matter where you are or what you do in life this book can help you to inevitably become a leader. Remember: it is never too late to become a leader. As in every tree there is a forest, so in every follower there is a leader.

Becoming A Leader Workbook
by Myles Munroe

Now you can activate your leadership potential through the *Becoming A Leader Workbook*. This workbook has been designed to take you step by step through the leadership principles taught in *Becoming A Leader*. As you participate in the work studies in this workbook you will see the true leader inside you develop and grow into maturity. *"Knowledge with action produces results."*

Mobilizing Human Resources

by Richard Pinder

Pastor Pinder gives an in-depth look at how to organize, motivate, and deploy members of the Body of Christ in a manner that produces maximum effect for your ministry. This book will assist you in organizing and motivating your troops for effective and efficient ministry. It will also help the individual believer in recognizing their place in the body, using their God given abilities and talents to maximum effect.

The Minister's Topical Bible

by Derwin Stewart

The Minister's Topical Bible covers every aspect of the ministry providing quick and easy access to scriptures in a variety of ministry related topics. This handy reference tool can be effectively used in leadership training, counseling, teaching, sermon preparation, and personal study.

The Believers' Topical Bible

by Derwin Stewart

The Believers' Topical Bible covers every aspect of a Christian's relationship with God and man, providing biblical answers and solutions for all challenges. It is a quick, convenient, and thorough reference Bible that has been designed for use in personal devotions and group Bible studies. With over 3,500 verses systematically organized under 240 topics, it is the largest devotional-topical Bible available in the New International Version and the King James Version.

The Layman's Guide to Counseling

by Susan Wallace

The increasing need for counseling has caused today's Christian leaders to become more sensitive to raise up lay-counselors to share this burden with them. Jesus' command is to "set the captives free." *The Layman's Guide to Counseling* shows you how. A number of visual aids in the form of charts, lists, and tables are also integrated into this reference book: the most comprehensive counseling tool available. *The Layman's Guide to Counseling* gives you the knowledge you need to use advanced principles of Word-based counseling to equip you to be effective in your counseling ministry. **Topics Include** • Inner Healing • Parenting • Marriage • Deliverance • Abuse • Forgiveness • Drug & Alcohol Recovery • Youth Counseling • Holy Spirit • Premarital Counseling

Available at your local bookstore or by contacting:

Pneuma Life Publishing
P.O. Box 10612
Bakersfield, CA 93389-0612

1-800-727-3218
1-805-324-1741